DATE DUE

102			
Apr 30 76			
104			
May 19 76			
Geiger 8			
Tyo.			
T5			
GAYLORD			PRINTED IN U.S.A.

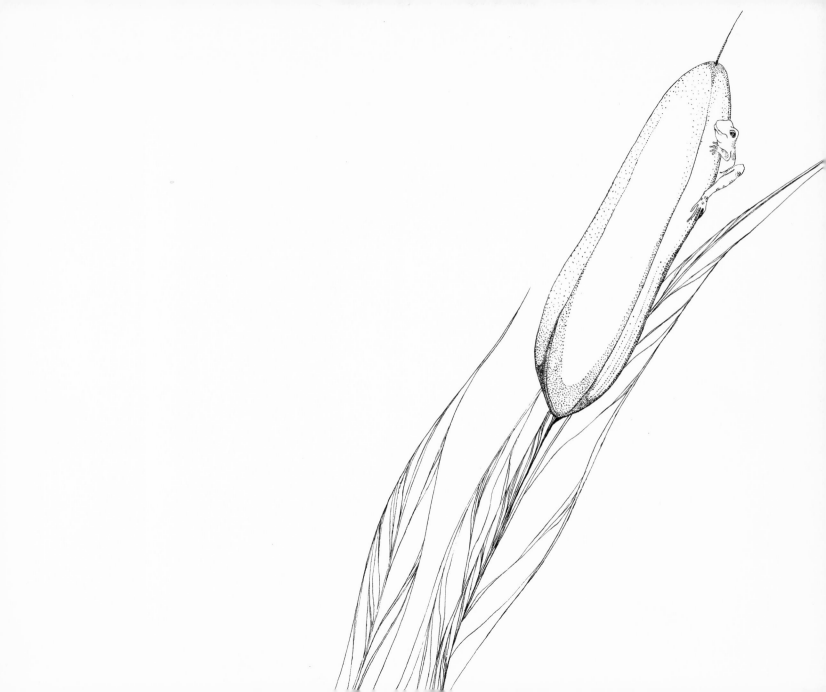

YEAR ON
MUSKRAT MARSH

by Berniece Freschet

Illustrated by Peter Parnall

CHARLES SCRIBNER'S SONS, NEW YORK

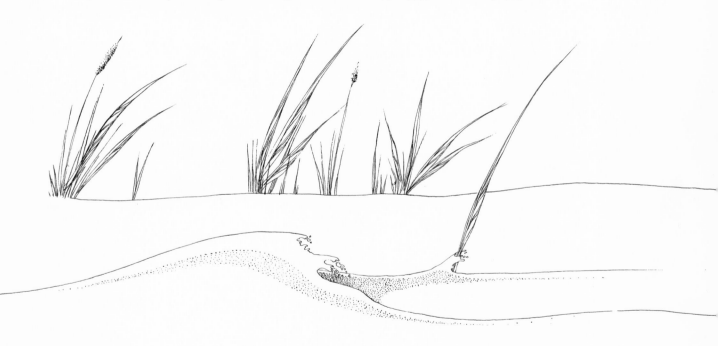

For Ferruccio,
    with love

INTRODUCTION

Among the many lakes and shallows sprinkled across northern Minnesota's wilderness area is the wetland—Muskrat Marsh.

Long ago this marsh was a lake. But generations of submerged water weeds raised the muddy bottom, and slowly a tangle of vegetation crept out from the lake shore. Then sedges and sphagnum moss made a thick mat of floating plants.

Now the water all around and underneath this garden is gradually filling in with more plants and silt and mud. And one day, Muskrat Marsh will have disappeared.

In this half-wet, half-dry world, creatures of the marshland come on swift wings, swooping down to the water. They come on webbed feet, splashing near the reeds. They come thirsty, trudging along well-worn paths. They come to the marsh, and all depend on it for life.

It was a hot July day at Muskrat Marsh. Not a breeze stirred through the leaves or grasses. Large white clouds drifted slowly overhead, and lily blossoms filled the warm air with their sweet smell. Insects hummed drowsily.

A red-winged blackbird perched on a cattail and sang a song, while long-legged striders skated upon the smooth water as if in rhythm to his music. They skimmed across the marsh making tiny, round dimples on its glassy surface.

Splash! Splash! Splash!

Three young muskrats dived into the water. Then they pulled themselves back up on their raft of mud and sticks and took turns diving into the marsh.

On a fallen log that jutted halfway into the water, a big bullfrog lay as if asleep. This was his favorite sunning place, and he came often to enjoy the warmth of the noonday sun.

He was one of the oldest and largest of the bullfrogs—the grandfather of them all here at the marsh. Only the moss-backed snapping turtle and the old water snake had lived here longer than he.

The bullfrog had grown very big. His body was over eight inches long and his powerful hind legs were over ten inches. He was an excellent swimmer—his strong legs and webbed feet pushed him through the water almost as well as the fins of a fish. He had recently shed his skin, and now his new green coat was sleek and smooth.

The bullfrog's bulging eyes blinked, a mosquito floated near. . . .

He opened his great mouth and a sticky tongue darted out.

He swallowed his catch and stretched a long leg and settled himself more comfortably.

The old water snake also knew of the sunning place and glided silently, twisting through the lily pads and around the stalks of cattail.

Almost to the log, the snake stopped and carefully raised

his head out of the water. His flicking tongue tested the air for scent. He smelled frog. Slowly, slowly he inched closer.

His glistening body arched.

With lightning-like speed, he struck!

Splash! The big bullfrog jumped into the water and quickly swam away. This was not the first time these two had met—nor would it be the last.

The old water snake didn't try to follow. It would have been useless, and besides, he wasn't hungry. Yesterday he had eaten a meal of several tadpoles and two small fish. This would last him for almost a week. What he had really wanted was the sunning place.

He wriggled up on the log and stretched his chunky body almost to its full length. He came here every day when the weather was good, for he liked the warmth of the midday sun on his shiny scales.

The younger water snakes in the marsh were more brilliantly colored than he. With age, the water snake's upper body had dulled to a muddy brown color, but underneath he was still marked with dark red bands and splotches.

His wide head gave him a fierce look, and he resembled his cousin, the deadly water moccasin of the southern marshes. But he was not a poisonous snake and was dangerous only to frogs, small fish, tadpoles, and water creatures that lived in the marsh.

The warm sun and his full stomach made the old snake sleepy. He drowsed.

Under the heat of the sun, it seemed as if all the creatures of the marsh were napping.

The muskrats had gone to their burrows in the bank.

A family of wood ducks glided by the log where the old water snake lay dozing. The mother duck, her neck stretched forward, led the brood of six youngsters across the water, while the father brought up the rear, keeping guard.

In the beginning eleven ducks had hatched, but the snapping turtle, the mink, and other enemies had already taken five of them. They stopped to feed. Standing on their heads with feathered bottoms pointing skyward, they nibbled on the tender shoots of pond plants and water weeds.

High above, a bald eagle hung motionless against the blue sky. His keen eyes searched the ground below. He was hunting food for the two hungry young eaglets back in his nest. He saw the family of young ducks and quickly folded his wings against his body. Swiftly, silently, he plunged downward.

The old water snake, suddenly aware of the dark shadow

passing overhead, dropped into the water. There he was safe, but on land he was exposed to his enemies. He must always be on guard for eagles and hawks, owls and weasels, and sometimes even other snakes.

The father duck also saw the shadow, and he quacked a warning.

The family scuttled under low-hanging willow boughs and hid among the rushes that grew at the water's edge. But one of the ducklings did not move fast enough.

The bald eagle flashed down, sunlight glinting on his sharp talons. He scooped up the duckling and, with a harsh scream, rose into the sky, soon disappearing in the white clouds high above.

Now only five ducklings were left.

The mother duck called her family together.

They glided close to a tall bird standing silently on one long stilt-leg, the other drawn close against his body hidden under his feathers. His long neck was twined backward and his head snugly tucked under a wing. The great blue heron was taking a nap.

The ducks paddled by the heron and swam toward a big moose feeding on submerged plants and weeds. The moose lifted his head and snorted. Streamers of water weeds hung from his great antlers like long ribbons of green velvet.

Content, he chewed his food, paying little attention to the approaching convoy.

Unafraid, the duck family swam by the great moose, on through a patch of wild rice, and beyond the muskrats' raft of mud and sticks to the far side of the marsh.

A black nose rippled the water. A young muskrat pulled himself up onto his raft and dived off. Two other young muskrats followed. They swam to the marsh bottom, where they dug in the mud for roots of arrowhead and cattail. They carried these back to the surface and climbed up on their stick island. Here they sat, and with their sharp teeth they munched on thick, white root bulbs. This was their favorite food, but they also ate frogs, tadpoles, clams, and small fish.

Even though they were young muskrats, born only this spring, they had already almost reached their full growth. In water their long, flat, scaly tails and webbed hind feet made them excellent swimmers, but on land they were slower and easily caught. So the muskrats built rafts of sticks and cattail stems mixed with mud and anchored these to the plants in the water. These platforms became their feeding and sunning places.

Now two of the muskrats dived off the raft and swam away, leaving their brother behind to keep watch. They swam a short distance out and joined another muskrat at a mound of mud, rushes, and cattail stalks. This was their winter home. During the summer they lived in deep burrows dug into the banks at the water's edge. But in a few months, when the nights grew

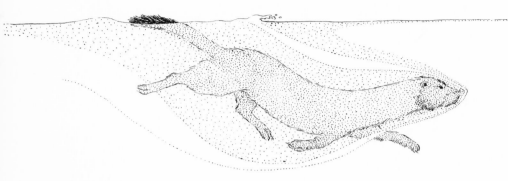

frosty, they would move out of their burrows and into their bigger and warmer house.

The little animals were busy repairing their lodge, making it ready for winter. Like the beavers, the muskrats were tireless workers. They brought stalks, leaves, and marsh grass, which they mixed with mud, and covered over the mound. Inside the mound was a hollowed-out room. Two tunnels led from this chamber into the water. It was a fine house.

While the family worked together, the young muskrat on the raft kept a careful lookout for enemies. He sat very still, watching and listening for any sign of danger. He saw a large ripple on the water. Then a sleek, black head rose up.

It was their enemy—the mink.

Whack! The muskrat dived, his tail hitting the water.

The others heard the warning, and they too dived, disappearing underwater. Swiftly they swam into the tunnels that led to their dug-out homes in the bank.

The mink heard the whack of the muskrat's tail and his bright eyes looked eagerly about. He swam toward the bank but he could not find the muskrats' burrows, and for now they were safe.

On the lily leaf squatted the big bullfrog—alert—ready to leap in an instant if the mink turned his way.

A purple dragonfly darted near the old water snake, who

lay hidden among the floating duck weed, watching. The mink swam near. The snake lay still.

Nothing was safe from the hungry mink—anything that moved in the water was his prey. His sharp teeth gripped a wiggling salamander.

"Caw! Caw! Caw!" cried a crow overhead.

The mink swam through the bulrushes and headed for shore where he could eat his meal in a secluded place—away from watching eyes.

"Caw! Caw!" The crow flapped away to the meadow to feast on the huckleberries that had begun to ripen.

In August not many birds came to the marsh. They had raised their young and it was now molting time. At this uncomfortable period, most of the birds hid themselves away in the woods.

It was a quiet time now at the marsh. Meadow grasshoppers and cicadas made soft music during the day, while field and tree crickets and katydids sang at night.

Berries ripened. Blackberries, blueberries, gooseberries, chokecherries, currants, wild strawberries and raspberries grew heavy and sweet with their juices. It would not be long before the great migration of birds would come from the north and gorge themselves on the plump, ripe berries. Some of the shore-birds had already started on their way south, and soon the warblers from Canada would come flying in during the nights.

Leopard and pickerel frogs, which had been tadpoles only a few weeks ago, now emerged from the marsh full-grown. Their new coats were beautifully marked and colored with yellows and browns. The pickerel frog would spend most of his life on shore, but he would never wander more than a half dozen hops away from the safety of the water.

However, the leopard frog was a great traveler, making long treks overland to live in almost any spot that was damp.

Day followed day, and it was not long before the hot, sticky days of August faded into the warm, golden days of September.

Late one afternoon, a mother black bear and her two cubs came out of the woods looking for food. The three fat, woolly bears soon found the patch of sweet gooseberries and sat down to enjoy the feast.

For the rest of the afternoon they squatted, pushing the juicy berries into their mouths, moving only when they were tempted to try the next bush. Finally, as the late afternoon sun slid below the hill, the mother bear struggled to her feet, and grunting her contentment, she waddled away from the sumptuous feast, leading her cubs back to their den in the woods.

The sky turned a soft blue. It was dusk—a time for new life to come to the marsh. Perched on a tree stump, a bird whistled softly. "Whip-poor-will . . .Whip-poor-will."

A mother deer and her fawn stepped out of the trees. For a moment they stood knee-deep in the meadow grass, alert, their ears twitching nervously. The doe nuzzled her fawn, and then with dainty steps they moved cautiously toward the marsh. They had come for their evening drink.

From the woods, the clear sweet song of the hermit thrush drifted through the twilight. A sudden sharp crack of a dead branch broke the evening's quiet.

The deer and her fawn bounded away. Across the meadow they flew and with a flick of their stubby white tails were gone, back to the safety of the woods.

A killdeer flew up, crying his name, "Kildee! Kildee!"

Later, as the creatures of the day snuggled into their warm beds to sleep, the creatures of the night awakened.

Crickets filled the air with soft chirping, and from the trees and marsh, sounded the chorus of frogs.

The old water snake pushed through the dark waters looking for a place to spend the night.

The great horned owl awoke, blinked his eyes, and ruffled his feathers. He stretched leg and wing. With a hungry snap of his beak, he sprang from his tree branch and on silent wings flew to the meadow to look for mice.

A fat skunk wiggled out of a hollow log and waddled down a beaten path to the marsh. On his way he turned over rocks and pieces of wood, looking for grasshoppers, grubs, and beetles to eat.

September was the time of great bird migrations, and the month of the harvest moon. Soon the moon rose, round and golden. During the night great flocks of birds swept across its bright face. Shorebirds—snipe, cranes, loons. Land birds—swallows, robins, warblers. Thousands of birds swooping and swirling, all winging their way south.

On their long journey many stopped at the marsh to find food and a safe place to rest. Honking loudly, a Canada gander and his family flew low. With legs thrust forward and wild flapping of wings, the big birds alighted on the water. Another family followed, and a pair of snow geese glided down. The marsh became a noisy refuge.

Pale moonlight shone across the marsh, making a sparkling path over the water. The cattails stood tall and black against the sky.

Two young raccoons ambled down a smooth path on their way to the marsh to hunt for frogs, snails, and small fish. They crept out on a large flat rock near the water's edge. Skillfully they dipped their slender paws in and out of the water.

In one quick, smooth motion the littlest raccoon's paw flashed down and come up clutching a dripping snail. She cracked the shell with her sharp teeth and then swished the

snail around in the water. She sucked the sweet morsel, smacking her lips.

After the raccoons had eaten their fill of snails and crayfish, they licked their paws and washed their faces. In a little while they ambled back along the pathway.

When he was sure that it was safe, the big bullfrog jumped from his hiding place under a fern and onto the rock. He looked down at the water and saw a familiar, long body go twisting by. His bulging eyes watched until the old water snake disappeared into a tangle of pond weeds. Hidden here, the snake spent the night.

From the meadow came the hunting cry of the great horned owl. The frog hunched forward—ready to spring to safety.

A small family of wood mice scurried across the pathway.

In the dark sky above, a lone mallard drake banked his glide and splashed down. The sudden sound startled the bullfrog, and he leaped from the rock. Under the water his strong legs thrust him deep and deeper—down, down to the muddy bottom of the marsh. He squatted among the twisting roots and weeds, and here, safely hidden, he rested.

The stars grew dim. In the east the horizon slowly began

to change from black to gray. The sky grew lighter, and gradually a hush fell over the marshland.

In that still moment between darkness and dawn, all life
stood motionless—waiting, listening.

From out of a tangle of cattails, a bittern lifted up into the
air, uttering his hoarse cry. He had been standing so still, with
his long beak pointing skyward, that he had looked like a clump
of cattails. His sudden departure startled a family of jays, and
they scolded angrily.

Singing joyously, a flock of redwinged blackbirds flew out
of the reeds and swooped away to the meadow.

The sky turned pink. In a sudden flash, the sun burst over
the rim of the horizon, shining across the marshland. White
clouds of mist drifted up from the water.

A new day had begun at the marsh.

The days grew shorter and the nights colder.

By the end of September frost had lightly brushed her fall colors across the land. The chokecherries were the first to show a flush in their leaves.

The tamarack tree turned a soft golden color, and the sumacs and swamp maples became a fiery red. With its bright oranges, yellows, and reds, the marsh looked aflame.

With October came falling leaves, ripening nuts, and the first of the killing frosts. Soon the last of the summer flowers faded, and the leafy ferns turned brown.

It was time for the muskrats to move out of their burrows

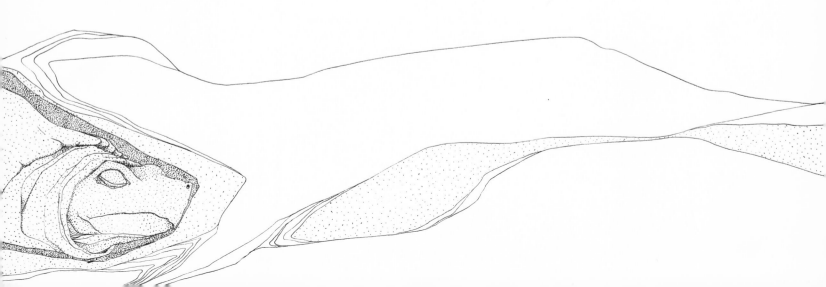

in the bank and into their warm lodge. Some hibernators had already begun their long winter nap.

Frogs and toads were asleep—the big bullfrog lay cozy in the mud at the bottom of the marsh.

The snapping turtle had made his home in the thick ooze, and many of the water bugs and insects also hid themselves away for the winter.

The old water snake, feeling the autumn chill, moved sluggishly through the water. It was not long before he too burrowed into the mud for a long sleep.

The sap and juices of the trees and bushes withdrew from

stems and branches and were now stored in roots and bulbs, where they would stay until the coming of spring. Life had slowed down and was even suspended for many of the plants and animal life here.

The marsh grew quiet.

The tamarack trees dropped their needles and stood tall and stark against the grey sky. Cold winds blew down from the north, whistling through the bare boughs.

In November, a thin skim of ice formed along the edge of the marsh, moving further outward each day.

The skunk pushed his round body into a hole at the base of a dead tree stump. He shouldered his way down a tunnel and into a scooped-out den lined with grass and leaves. He wedged himself in between two other friendly skunks, and here, together, the fat furry companions would sleep through most of the winter.

The raccoon was also ready for her nap, and she climbed the maple tree. She squeezed through the opening and down to her nest in the hollow below. Soon she was joined by another raccoon.

Neither the skunks nor the raccoons slept too soundly, and in the winter months ahead they would often awake and come out for short prowls about the countryside. But they never strayed too far, nor did they linger for too long away from the comfort of their warm, dark beds.

A white flurry of snow whirled across the marshland.

Now ice covered all the water and with each passing day grew thicker.

Even the black bear knew that it was time to find shelter from the cold. She took her cubs deep inside a cave, and the three snuggled down together. The stored fat in their bodies would last them for many months.

The temperature dropped below zero. Gusts of cold wind swept across the land.

Winter had come to the marsh.

The mink was hungry!

A shrew ran out from under a bush and instantly the mink pounced. This was his last meal at the marsh. He started for the big river. In the spring he would return.

Blizzard winds howled over the marshland.

The old water snake and the bullfrog burrowed deeper into the mud.

It was a time of great hardship for the deer, the mouse, and the rabbit, and all animals who had to forage through the snow to find food.

For them it was a fierce battle to stay alive.

One morning a muskrat pushed his nose out of a bubble hole at the edge of one of his rafts. He climbed up on the ice and munched on a stalk, keeping a sharp lookout for enemies. The hungry fox or owl would relish a breakfast of muskrat.

From a clear, blue sky, the sun shone down, making the snowy countryside sparkle.

A group of noisy tree sparrows called from the birches.

A grey squirrel ran down a tree and scampered across the marsh, scattering bright snow into the air.

Overhead a flock of snowbirds winged by.

Not far from the muskrats' lodge, snowprints showed that

a fox had recently visited the lodge. He had stopped awhile to sniff the tantalizing odor of the rat inside, then followed the snowprints of a cottontail.

A wood mouse scurried across the marsh, his dainty footprints lacing the snow. From a pine tree at the edge of the marsh, an owl leaped far out—the dark shadow of his wings skimming over the white ground below. He swooped low—

Abruptly the mouse's footprints ended.

A few grey hairs, three tiny red spots, and the mark of an owl's wing tips told a winter's story written on the snow.

The snow was still deep in February, but the arrival of the little woodcock, flying in from the warm south, gave the marshland its first hint that spring was on its way. The woodcock was one of the earliest of the spring birds to return to the north.

Toward the end of February, a green pointed bud pushed up through the snow. It was a skunk cabbage—the first flower of spring. Soon large cabbage-like leaves unfurled. The big bud thickened into a purple hood speckled with greenish yellow spots. Inside the hood, on a long stem, was a round knob covered with tiny flowers. Flies and insects filled the hood, buzzing around the first flower of spring.

Deep in the woods the mother bear awakened. She yawned and stretched, and then she took her two new cubs out into the sunlight. For the first couple of days the bear ate nothing, but then she smelled the strong odor of the skunk cabbage. It looked very appetizing, and she soon began to tear at the juicy roots and tender green leaves, not caring that the skunk cabbage tasted bitter.

Warm breezes blew across the marsh, melting patches of ice and snow. Sap rose in the dogwood and maple, turning the marsh shores almost as red as they had been last autumn. Buds swelled out on the poplar and willow stems.

In some places, open water showed. Striders, beetles, and swarms of insects quickly gathered.

The old water snake pushed out of his bed of mud and twisted sluggishly upward. He swam to a thick clump of grasses and slowly pulled himself up onto the hummock to lie and wait for the pale sun to warm his torpid body.

One bright March morning the blackbirds flew in.

Their gay wing patches of red and yellow flashed across the marshland as they filled the air with their cheery songs.

Big bullfrogs bellowed. . . .

"JUG-O-RUM—JUG-O-RUM." It seemed as though the whole marsh was singing, "It's spring! It's spring!"

April rains melted the last of the snow and ice.

All the land turned green.

At first the rains fell gently upon the marsh, riffling the water. Then the sky grew black and the wind howled. Soon a gale whipped across the wetland, swaying and tossing the willows and cattails and churning the water into foaming whitecaps.

A grey sheet of rain poured down.

The little woodcock huddled in her nest.

A fox hurried home to his den, not even looking at the rabbit nearby who quickly disappeared into his hole.

Everywhere marsh creatures scurried for shelter from the storm.

All night it rained, and all the next day—and the next. The log where the snake and the bullfrog liked to sun themselves was now underwater.

The muskrat family sat on top of their stick house and watched the water lapping higher and higher. They huddled close together. Six new tiny babies clung to their mother's fur.

A nest full of goose eggs floated by.

Seeking shelter, the old water snake swam near and pulled himself up on the muskrats' lodge.

Already hidden there among the twisted sticks, the big bullfrog watched with bulging eyes.

A sudden surge of water pushed against the muskrats' house. The lodge tipped to the side. Another swell broke it loose from its foundation.

The muskrat family clung together as their floating home tossed and turned upon the water.

Many homes were destroyed by the storm.

The muskrat lodge floated past a tree stump where a skunk hunched forward, looking down at the swirling waters around him.

A tree floated by. A white-footed mouse clung tight to a branch, while on a limb two sparrows huddled close to their nest.

The muskrats' stick house bobbed across the water. The babies held tight to their mother.

A sleek head rose out of the water—the mink had returned. He swam toward the muskrats' lodge.

The mother muskrat stood up on her hind legs; she hissed a warning, showing sharp, pointed teeth. She was a fierce fighter—especially dangerous when she had new babies.

The mink knew this and, seeing the fury of the mother muskrat, he wisely turned and swam away.

Gradually the wind quieted.

The next morning the rains stopped, and soon patches of blue sky showed. Through the dark scattered clouds, a warm, bright ray of sunlight shone down.

The muskrats dived off their floating home and swam to the shore where they would build new burrows in the banks.

The bullfrog leaped and with a splash was gone.

The dark shadowy form of the old water snake twisted slowly away, through the now still waters of the marsh.

The storm had passed. The danger was over.

Slowly the rain waters receded and flowers bloomed.

Marsh marigolds and tiny, sky-blue forget-me-nots blossomed at the edge of the marsh. Sweet white violets nestled against the earth.

The days grew warmer.

Ferns pushed up through the thick mat of grasses and slowly unfolded their lacy, green fiddleheads to the warm air.

Algae turned the water green.

These floating plants provided the food for the hundreds of tiny, nibbling, wiggling water-life—the tadpoles, pollywogs, and minnows; the water bugs, mosquitoes, fleas, and countless numbers of other small insects and larvae which swam all around. In turn, many of these became food for the pickerel, bass, and perch; the birds, the frogs, and the water snakes; and all the many forms of life that existed in and around the wetland.

May was a time of new life, the month when young things were born. Baby ducks and goslings pecked their way out of shell walls and followed their parents, swimming behind them on the water.

One morning, mother muskrat swam out of her burrow, her youngsters following.

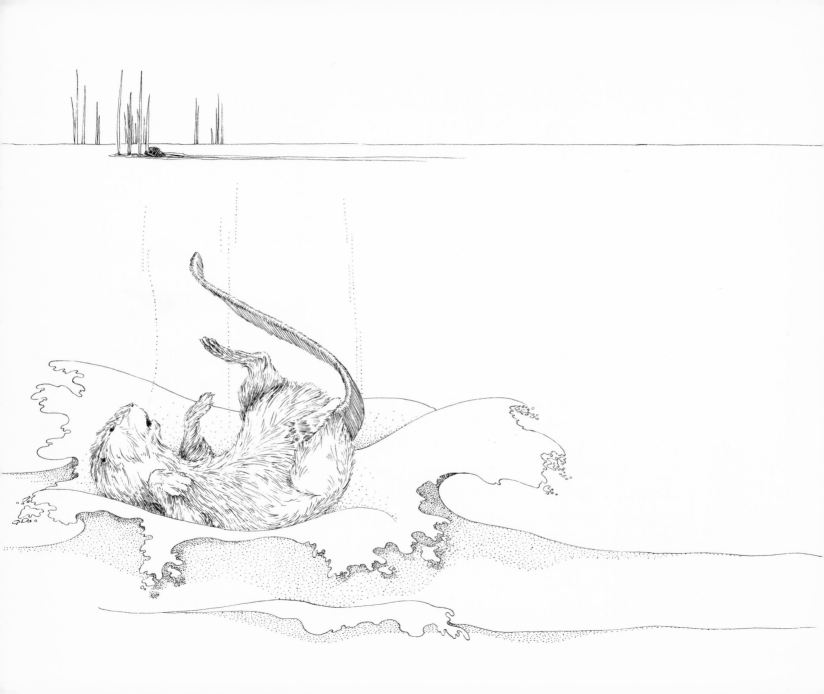

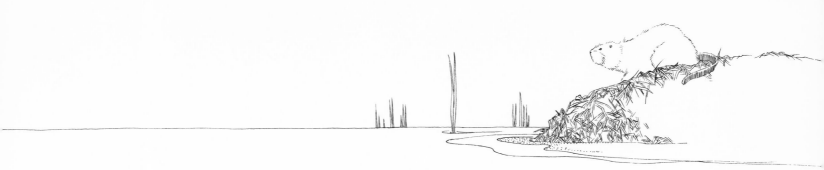

The little muskrats were not even half grown, but from now on they must take care of themselves. They had no fear, for they still had to learn that in their world there were many enemies to watch out for.

They crawled onto a raft of cattail stalks and shook themselves. They were hungry and began to nibble on the new, green shoots they found there. A dark shadow passed overhead, but they paid no attention.

A young hawk swiftly dived.

Sharp talons gripped one of the muskrats.

The little muskrat squalled in fear, kicking the air.

The young hawk, being new at the business of hunting, had misjudged his dive and did not have a firm grip.

The squirming muskrat fell free, splashing into the water below.

From now on the young muskrats would keep a careful lookout for enemies.

In June the turtles crawled out of the marsh and looked for dry, sandy places to lay their eggs. They dug hollows in the sand, and into these scooped-out bowls they laid their eggs and covered them with dirt.

When the eggs hatched the little turtles instinctively knew that they must scramble to the water as fast as they could.

One twilight evening, the soft, clear call of the whippoor-will again drifted across the marshland.

A new generation of young had begun its cycle of life.

The days grew hot and hotter.

Every day the bullfrog and the old water snake swam to their favorite log to stretch themselves and bask lazily in the warm sun.

Once again the marsh grew quiet, and life drowsed under the shimmering heat of summertime.

Another July had come.